PROJECT MANAGEMENT

Proven Project Management And Project Planning Techniques To Complete Any Project Succesfully!

Henry Hubbard

Table of Contents

Table of Contents

Introduction

Chapter 1: Understanding Project Management
Defining a Project
Stages of a Project
Defining Project Management
Project Management Processes

Chapter 2: Project Selection and Prioritization
The Strategic Management Process
Why You Need a Project Selection and Prioritization Mechanism
The Project Selection and Prioritization Process
Project Selection Approaches

Chapter 3: Planning your Project Effectively
The Project Scope Statement
Justifying Your Project
Getting Your Project Objectives Right
Dealing with Project Constraints

Chapter 4: Project Scheduling
Planning the Schedule
Controlling the Work
How to Manage Your Project Schedule

Chapter 5: Managing Project Risks
Risk Management
Risk Factors
Risk Identification
Risk Evaluation
Estimating the Consequences

The Risk Management Strategy
The Risk-Management Plan

Chapter 6: Resource Management, Planning, and Budgeting
Resource Allocation and Management
Resource Planning
Resource Budgeting

Chapter 7: Picking the Right Project Team
The PAC Principle
The Generalizing Specialist
Team Chemistry
Qualities of a Project Team Member

Chapter 8: Defining Roles and Responsibilities
Understanding Project Roles
Handling Project Assignments

Chapter 9: Evaluating Project Results
Ongoing Project Evaluation
Measuring your Project's Results

Chapter 10: Reporting Project Status
The Management Perspective
Issue Management

Chapter 11: Closing the Project
Planning For Closure
Dealing with Administrative Issues
Transitioning your team members
Post-Project Review
The Evaluation Meeting

Chapter 12: Project Management Challenges and Failures

Top 10 Project Management Challenges
Ten Major Causes of Project Failure

Chapter 13: Ten Tips for Successful Project Management

Conclusion

Introduction

Project management is not a new term or concept. As long as there have been projects, there has always been some form of project management. Looking back throughout history, there is plenty of evidence of projects, large and small, being undertaken by human beings. Some of these projects were construction oriented, artistic masterpieces, literary works or even medical revolutions.

If project management has been around for so long, why are people still interested in this subject to this day? The truth is that the way projects are handled has changed tremendously and the people who manage the projects have also evolved in their thinking based on experiences and new innovative methods introduced in this and the last century.

In this book, *"Project Management: Proven Project Management And Project Planning Techniques To Complete Any Project Succesfully!,"* you will get to fully appreciate what project management is all about. This book will break down the core elements of project management and build them back up in a way that makes the subject relevant to the 21st century.

People tend to have diverse perspectives of what project management really is and how to go about it. There are numerous elements that make up a successful project, and every great project manager must learn how to identify these elements and get them to work together. The difference between project success and failure in today's world can come down to paying attention to the nitty-gritty details.

This book will help you understand the basic concepts

relating to the art and science of project management. The information presented is simple and easy to apply. Though there may be some technical and analytical content, you will still be able to master it within a short time. Pay close attention to the critical tools and techniques explained in the book. You will need them to support your planning, organizing, scheduling, staffing, budgeting and controlling those processes that make up the projects you are expected to handle.

This book defines project management, teaches you how to plan the process, and how to manage a project team effectively. Everything you need to know about a project, from design to closure, is covered here. You will also learn about some of the common challenges that project managers face in their work, as well as things that are likely to make your project end in failure. If you are managing any kind of project, this information will open your eyes and help you achieve the success of your project!

Chapter 1: Understanding Project Management

The first step in understanding what project management actually entails is to clarify what a project is and what its components are. If you perform some kind of work on a daily basis, then you probably handle different kinds of assignments. Every project is an assignment, but not all assignments can be classified as a project. So how do we know what a project is?

Defining a Project

Many different authors have come up with various definitions of a project. Let us take a look at some of them.

According to UNCRD (2000), a project can be defined as a group of complex activities that consume resources with the expectation that returns will be realized. These activities require planning, financing, and implementing. A project must have specific time constraints (start and end point) as well as specific objectives. The benefits of a project must also be identifiable, quantifiable, and socially or financially valuable.

According to ISO 10006, a project can be defined as a unique process made up of planned and controlled activities with start and end dates, undertaken to achieve a specific objective through the use of resources.

Cleland and Ireland (2007) define a project as a set of organizational resources brought together to create a product or service that was not in existence previously, in order to provide the capacity to design and execute organizational strategies. A project must also have a distinct life cycle.

From the above definitions of a project, it is clear to see that certain concepts keep popping up. A project must fulfill specific objectives, involve specific activities designed to fulfill those objectives (scope of work), have a specific start and end point (schedule), and involve utilization of resources (people, finances, raw materials, e.t.c.) A project is, therefore, a unique endeavor that involves particular activities, designed to achieve specific objectives within a specific timeframe, using defined resources, and carrying an element of risk.

From this definition, a project can be any activity, ranging from the construction of a road, developing software, releasing a new product onto the market and even strategically planning disaster relief efforts. To be successful, all these activities require project management.

Stages of a Project

Regardless of the nature or size of a project, there are four general stages that it will have to go through:

1. **Project initiation stage** – This involves developing, assessing and framing the need for the project, deciding how it will be undertaken and agreeing on the need for a definite plan. Approvals are obtained, rough estimates of the resources required are drawn up, and the key personnel required are listed.

2. **Project organizing stage** – This involves creating a detailed project plan that clarifies the goals and objectives, the activities to be undertaken, the budget, timeframe, and other resources required and a risk management plan.

3. **Project execution stage** – This involves gathering a project team, setting up project support structures, executing the activities outlined in the plan and controlling performance to make sure that objectives are being achieved. This stage normally produces outputs such as progress reports or results.

4. **Project closing stage** – This involves evaluating the results of the project, moving the team on to new assignments, closing financial accounts and undertaking a post-project evaluation. This is the stage where the project results are approved, lessons learned are reviewed, and recommendations made on how to improve future projects.

Defining Project Management

Project management can be defined as the process of pulling together the required resources – expertise, labor, skills, tools, finances, materials, etc. – to achieve the objectives of a project as per the requirements. It can also be described as the process of guiding a project from inception through its performance to closure.

From this definition, it is clear to see that project management is something that most people may have been engaged in at one point in time, even if it was informal in nature. There are generally five sets of processes that make up project management. These processes are somewhat similar to the project stages discussed in the previous section. They provide support to the various stages of a project and are performed in a cyclic manner that ensures project activities run as required.

In order to undertake these project management processes successfully, a project manager must have three things:

- **Information** – Your information has to be timely, accurate and complete. The data you are working with will be used when planning, monitoring performance and assessing the final results of every activity in relation to the intended objectives.

- **Communication skills** – You must be able to clarify information, practice openness and share data with team members and stakeholders in a timely manner.

- **Commitment** – Every team member must be committed to doing everything to ensure that the project objectives are achieved on schedule and within budget.

Project Management Processes

The initiating process

Every project starts out as an idea. It could be a need that has been identified, a new market that has little competition, or simply a strategy to improve an existing process with an organization.

The initiating process is usually a formal one that involves reviewing the proposal and getting approval to proceed from top management. However, it can sometimes be tailored to suit a smaller, more informal project, thus requiring a simple verbal commitment.

When the decision makers sit down to determine whether to initiate a project or not, they have to look at two key issues:

- The cost-benefit ratio – Will the benefits be worth the resources invested?

- The feasibility of the project - Is the project financially and technically feasible?

Unless both issues can be resolved and the questions answered with a firm "Yes," the project cannot be initiated. The decision makers can decide to make the project more beneficial and feasible, but if it is not possible to do so, then it should be canceled. There is no need to waste valuable resources that can be channeled elsewhere on a project that isn't worth the investment.

A cost-benefit analysis is a very important tool during the project initiating process. It is a comparative evaluation of the benefits and costs of a particular project. A cost-benefit analysis can help you to:

- Determine whether to start a project

- Determine which of several projects should be undertaken

- Know how to design project objectives

- Estimate how much resources will be required to make the project a success

The planning process

Now that the initiating process is over and the project has been deemed beneficial and feasible, it is time to prepare a detailed plan. The planning process also involves detailing how your project team will actualize the plan. The project management plan should include the following information:

- Reasons for undertaking the project

- The specific project objectives

- The constraints that need to be addressed

- All the assumptions that relate to the project

- All the project activities involved

- A description of the roles and responsibilities of every team member

- A detailed project schedule

- An estimate of the financial, personnel, and material resources required

- A risk management plan

- A strategy for how team members will communicate and stay updated

- A strategy for ensuring progress is monitored and quality is controlled

It is important to note that a project plan is always more effective when it is written down. The size of the project does not matter. Writing things down always reveals some of the elements you may have forgotten as well as clarifying details further. Whether a project is successfully executed may come down to how clear and accurate the plan is and whether the team members believe that it is achievable. At this stage, it is very important not to leave out any stakeholder because you will need their full commitment to make the project a success.

There are some project managers who face intense pressure to start a project and complete it quickly. This forces them to skip the planning process and get down to the execution stage. Though this may seem like a good idea at first, especially if the project activities start to move quickly, there will be a lot of wastage, confusion, and mistakes down the road.

Always remember that getting written approval for the project plan is necessary. It may involve a short email or the document being signed by the person in charge. In most cases, especially in large projects, the plan has to be formally reviewed and approved by several individuals within the organization.

The execution process

Once you have come up with a detailed and written project plan, the execution phase can then be launched. The execution process normally involves specific tasks, such as:

- Linking every project role with a specific individual. Make sure that the people you have picked will be available when the project begins. In case you are borrowing people from different departments within the organization, you will have to talk their respective managers and negotiate with them.

- Gathering the team members and introducing them to one another. It is a good idea to help your team get to know one another well. This is also an opportunity for the team to get to understand and appreciate the project, its significance, its purpose, and support structures.

- Informing every team member of their tasks and explaining their specific responsibilities.

- Explaining to the team how the essential project functions will be carried out. For example, you need to define the communication methods that will be used to pass on information, the conflict resolution mechanisms, as well as any other important procedures.

- Establishing systems that will be used to monitor progress, expenditure, schedules, and e.t.c.

- Letting the project stakeholders know that the project has officially kicked off, what its objectives are, and the timeframe it has been given.

- Performing the activities defined within the project plan. As the project proceeds, you will be responsible for ensuring that the required quality standards are maintained, the team is managed well, and the information is shared in an effective and timely manner.

Monitoring and controlling process

Once a project has begun, you have to make sure that the project plan is being implemented and the intended results are being achieved. What do monitoring and controlling entail?

- Comparison of project performance with the plan – This involves gathering information about the results, achievements, and resource utilization. You should also identify any deviation from the plan and take corrective action if necessary.

- Identifying and resolving challenges – Reallocate resources and change tasks to ensure the performance of the project is aligned with its key objectives.

- Communicating with all stakeholders – Inform everyone concerned about project challenges, achievements, and any changes that have been made to the plan.

Closing process

Closing the project is more than just completing the assigned activities and walking away. There are some important tasks that have to be performed before the project can be considered officially closed. The closing process involves:

- Presenting the project results to the client for final approval.

- Closing your project accounts.

- Relocating and reassigning the team members to their new assignments.

- Inviting the project team to a post-project evaluation meeting where you celebrate achievements and discuss the lessons learned. This part is very important, so at least jot down some notes about what you learned and how that knowledge can be applied in future projects.

The above five processes are crucial to supporting the project as it progresses through its life cycle. The processes are not necessarily sequential, as a project manager may sometimes cycle back from executing to the planning process in case a problem arises and the plan needs modification. It is also important to note that the monitoring and controlling process is used in every stage of the project to make sure that the plan is on track.

Chapter 2: Project Selection and Prioritization

Most organizations today accept project management as the standard way of engaging in business. Projects are tools that an organization uses to implement their business strategy. It is, therefore, important to note that the way a project is managed will determine the level of productivity of the organization.

Every organization has a strategic plan that guides its activities, and therefore, every project that it engages in must contribute to this strategic plan. The challenge then is finding a way to make sure that there is a linkage between the two. This can only be done by integrating a project into the strategic plan. In other words, you have to make sure that projects are selected and prioritized according to the value they bring to the organization.

The Strategic Management Process

An organization always has a specific mission and goals

designed to meet the needs of the customers. The mission is usually what the organization wants to become, while the goals typically define the mission in terms of specific, tangible, and measurable terms. The reason why goals must be clearly defined is because they clarify the direction an organization is heading. There must be goals that set targets for every level within an organization. The goals can then be defined further into more detailed objectives.

When developing a strategy for how you are going to meet the customer's needs and reach organizational goals, the primary focus should be on the things that need to be done to make the goals a reality. This will require a broad analysis of the external and internal environments. The external environment can be analyzed by conducting a PEST (political, economic, social, and technological) analysis which will reveal potential threats and opportunities. The internal environment can be analyzed by searching for strengths and weaknesses, for example, core competencies, financial resources, management, and technology. The end product of these analyses is a set of strategies that will result in the needs of customers being met in the best possible way.

In order to implement these strategies, you will have to establish tasks and assignments. There are certain key points that you will also have to pay attention to:

- To effectively execute the tasks, there must be adequate resources, for example, funds, labor and equipment. The challenge here is that resources tend to be limited. Furthermore, having several different goals often leads to conflicting demands on the available resources. For this reason, there has to be a system put in place to prioritize the allocation of organizational resources.

- To effectively implement these strategies, there has to be structured support for projects from within the organization.

- Implementing strategies also requires project management processes to be used, such as planning, organizing, directing, and controlling.

- To ensure that a project is always linked to the organization's strategic plan, there must be a project selection and prioritization mechanism.

Why You Need a Project Selection and Prioritization Mechanism

- The organization may be trying to implement several different projects at the same time. It then becomes inevitable that at any given time, the number of projects in a portfolio will be more than the resources available.

- Every organization experiences some level of political maneuvering. This can affect the project selection and prioritization process in a massive way. There will always be some senior manager or executive who is pushing for their pet project to go through.

If you do not have an effective mechanism for selecting and prioritizing potential projects, the lack of available resources combined with political pressure may cause uncertainty, frustration, and wastage of resources.

Factors to consider for a project selection and prioritization mechanism

- How to reduce the influence of politics in determining which projects get chosen.

- How to ensure that priority is consistently given to projects that align with the organization's strategic plan.

- How to use the list of prioritized projects to allocate the limited resources available.

There will always be more project proposals than the organizational resources can handle. The mechanism to be used must select those projects that will consume resources and give a maximum return on value. You need to develop a decision model that uses carefully selected criteria.

These criteria are beneficial for the following reasons:

- They enable effective planning of resources

- They enable efficient use of resources

- They ensure the portfolio is comprised of projects that balance the threats and opportunities

- They ensure that stakeholders only pay attention to the most critical projects

- They help to achieve consensus around the high priority projects

It should be noted that it is normal to meet some kind of resistance when trying to institute a project selection and priority mechanism. This only indicates the serious need for such a system to be put in place. However, it is also crucial that you get the upper management to support the process of developing and implementing such a mechanism.

The Project Selection and Prioritization Process

There are a number of ways to select the best project out of many proposals and project ideas. In this section, you will learn about the preliminary screening method.

Preliminary screening

This involves eliminating any project ideas which do not seem promising on the surface. Preliminary screening usually involves looking into specific aspects, such as:

- **Project compatibility with the promoter** – The promoter simply refers to the individual who is interested in starting the project. It is important for the project idea to align with the interests, character, and resources of the promoter. The project that is selected must fit the personality of the promoter in terms of training, abilities, and inclinations. It is important that the project results in a considerable return on investment as well as provide opportunities for growth.

- **Project consistency with governmental**

priorities – There is a need to ensure that the project is within the government's national goals and regulatory framework. You will have to consider whether the project will result in any environmental effects that violate government regulations. There is also the issue of the complexity of getting a license for the project. This particular aspect is especially important if the project in question is being implemented by a foreign entity.

- **Availability of resources** – There must be adequate resources available for the project. Select a project whose capital requirements will be manageable and technical skills required are available. You must also consider whether the cost of raw materials is reasonable.

- **Market size** – Before you choose a project, you will have to consider whether the size of the market is big enough to assure you of a good return on investment. Some of the factors that you will need to consider include competitors and their market share, the size of the local market, your sale and distribution system, patent protection, social, economic and demographic trends, market entry barriers, the quality-price profile of the product, etc.

- **The cost of the project** - You need to ask yourself whether the proposed project has a reasonable cost structure. The profit to be realized from the endeavor must be acceptable. Some of the factors that influence the cost include labor, overheads, selling and distribution costs, administration expenses and service costs.

- **Risk level** – A project that has too much risk attached to it is not a good candidate for selection. Assessing the level of risk may be difficult, but there are certain factors that you can consider. These include technological changes; government regulations regarding pricing and distribution; competition from imported products; competition from substitute products; and susceptibility to business cycles.

Once you have seriously considered the above aspects of preliminary screening, you should construct a project rating index. This is a tool that is extremely useful in cases where an organization usually assesses several different project ideas at the same time. The project rating index makes the process of screening these projects easier. A project rating index is usually determined by:

- Identifying the factors that are appropriate for rating the project. Some of these have been mentioned above, for example, cost, availability of resources, market size, consistency with governmental priorities, e.t.c.

- Assigning weights to each factor such that each weight signifies the importance of the factor

- Rating the proposed project using an appropriate rating scale, based on either a 5-point or 7-point scale

- Multiply the rating and the weight for each factor to generate a factor score.

The task of determining the factor score for each project proposal is undertaken by a team that is set up specifically for this task. Those project proposals that have the highest factor score are the ones that will be considered for implementation.

Project Selection Approaches

There are two basic approaches that you can use to make decisions on which projects to implement. These are non-numeric and numeric approaches. Non-numeric approaches do not make use of any numerical values as inputs. These approaches have been around for longer and are simpler to use. Numeric approaches use numbers as inputs, but the criteria that are measured can either be objective or subjective.

Non-numeric approaches

1. **The sacred cow** – This approach is usually quite prevalent in organizations that have been in existence for a long time. The project ideas are proposed by the top hierarchy within the organization, and for this reason, projects are usually sparked by simple or casual statements to subordinates. A top manager may simply call a subordinate into their office and ask them to look into an idea that they have had, for example, the design of a new product or development of a new market. This approach is called "sacred" because the project must be implemented and completed successfully, or until the promoter of the idea realizes its weaknesses and kills the project.

2. **The operating necessity** – This is an approach that considers the proposed project to be of utmost importance and is absolutely necessary for the organization. For example, if a project is needed to streamline and upgrade the production system of a manufacturing company, then the decision makers will consider whether the production system is of importance to the organization. Since the production system is a vital cog in the operational survival of the organization, the project will be approved regardless of the cost. This does not mean that attempts will not be made to keep the costs as low as possible.

3. **The competitive necessity** – This is an approach that is used by organizations that want to maintain an edge of their industry rivals. These projects typically involve rebranding or modernization of projects that are already in existence. The decision makers realize that the organization must maintain its competitive position at all costs. This approach is usually very sophisticated. It is important to note that operating necessity is always considered weightier than competitive necessity.

4. **The product line extension** - This approach involves selecting a project based on how well its outcomes align with an organization's existing product line. For example, if the project is meant to develop and distribute a new product, the management will have to determine whether it strengthens the existing products, fills a gap, or takes the product line in a new direction with untapped potential. This approach does not always rely on perceptions of profitability. Upper management may

select a project based on how they believe the project will impact the total performance of the organization's system.

5. **The comparative benefit** – This is an approach that is used in situations where an organization is presented with several project ideas that do not have much in common. In other words, the projects being proposed cannot be compared directly to one another. For example, an organization may receive project proposals concerning the development of new products, changes in distribution methods, computerization of particular data, and even construction of a daycare center for personnel with babies. All these projects are totally different from each other and cannot be compared easily. The selection committee looks at all the project ideas and determines which one best fits the goals and budget of the organization. The project rating index can also be used to rank the projects and determine which one carries the greatest score. However, the decision on which project to select always takes into consideration the financial evaluation of each project proposed.

Numeric approaches

Most of the organizations that rely on numeric approaches for selection and prioritization of projects tend to view profitability as the most significant indicator of acceptability. These numeric approaches include:

1. **Inspection** – This approach is quite simple to use. You simply take the project proposals that have been submitted and calculate the net value of production of

each project over a span of, say, five years. The project that generates the greatest net value of production is considered the most profitable one to implement. In case you end up with several projects generating the same net value of production, you should select the project that produces benefits earlier than the others.

2. **Payback period** – This is the time span between the start of the project and when the net benefits start being realized. In other words, the payback period refers to how long it takes a project to return the capital invested and generate profits. This approach is most suitable for selecting projects with a business environment, more so where there is a high level of risk. The payback period approach is not very reliable and for this reason, it is normally supported by another numeric approach. It has two major weaknesses: It fails to take into account the money earned after the payback period, and it fails to take into account the differences in timing of earnings.

3. **Proceeds per dollar outlay** – This approach involves dividing the net value of production (total proceeds) by the total cost of investment (capital used). It has similar limitations as the payback period approach. It may also need to be supported by using another numeric approach.

4. **The average rate of return** – This is the ratio of average yearly profit to the initial investment made into the project. It is not considered to be an effective approach for selecting a project. However, it is a simple method of making project decisions.

5. **Cost-benefit ratio** – This approach is also known as profitability index. It is calculated by dividing the net present value of future cash flows by the initial capital invested. If the ratio is greater than 1.0, the project is considered for selection.

The process of selecting and prioritizing a project is a complex and delicate one. It is at this point that you must ensure that all the required data is available and the information you are using to make decisions is as precise as possible.

Chapter 3: Planning your Project Effectively

Projects are created for a specific reason. It is all about identifying a need and then trying to establish a structured mechanism for addressing that need. The success or failure of a project will depend on the extent to which it addresses that need. In order to plan a project effectively, you will have to develop a project scope statement.

The Project Scope Statement

The scope statement is a written record of the results a project is expected to generate and the conditions under which the project team will work. There must be an agreement between the project promoter/client and the project team regarding all the terms and conditions specified in the scope statement prior to the start of the project.

So what kind of information should you include in a scope statement?

- **Justification of the project** - This reveals the how and why of your project, the needs that it is supposed to address, the scope of work the project covers, and the relationship between the different project activities.

- **Objectives** - These are the project deliverables or results that are expected of the project.

- **Description of the product** – The functions and features of whatever results, products, or services the project will produce.

- **Criteria** for accepting the products

- **Constraints** – These are the things that will limit the intended results, how and when the results can be achieved, and the potential cost of the project.

- **Assumptions** – These are comments regarding what you will do to address uncertainties as the project is planned and undertaken.

The scope statement should be considered together with other elements of the project plan. This forms a binding agreement that commits you and your project team to producing the required results. All the restrictions and assumptions are agreed to by your team as well as the project promoters, who commit to supporting you according to the information in the scope statement. In case there are any assumptions that are invalidated, you can change some elements of the project plan.

There are a number of other documents that can be used in

place of a scope statement. They contain similar information to that in the scope statement. Of course, use of these documents depends on the type of organization, the kind of work it does, and the type of project being implemented. Some of these documents are:

- **Work order:** This is a document that specifies the work that various people will perform a part of the project, as well as the required work performance. It does not focus on project results.

- **Project charter:** This is a document written by senior management, formally creating a project and giving the project manager authority to utilize organizational resources to undertake the project.

- **Statement of work:** This is a document that specifies the results, products, and services that the project will produce.

- **Technical specifications document:** This document specifies the exact features that the product or service produced by the project must have.

- **Market requirements document:** This is usually drawn up by the sales and marketing department. It is a formal request to modify an existing product or create a new one.

- **Project profile:** This is also known as a project abstract. The document underlines key information about the project.

Justifying Your Project

If your project is to successfully meet the needs and expectations of the stakeholders involved, it is important to first understand the reasons why the project is being implemented. Most people may assume that they know the reasons for the project, but the question that must be answered is why the project is being done at all. The best way to answer this question is to identify the people who will benefit from the project and their needs and expectations.

Determining the project initiator

The project initiator is the person who first thought up the project. This is the person who had the original concept for the project. You need to identify this person and meet whatever needs and expectations they have.

If the person who conceived the project is the same person who assigned you the project, for example, your boss, then this becomes easy. However, as in most cases, the person who assigns you the project is simply a conduit. Your work becomes ever more complicated if the project idea passed through a chain of different people, potentially resulting in the original needs and expectations being altered or blurred.

In order to identify the project initiator, you should follow these steps:

1. Ask the person assigning the project if the idea was their own

2. If it wasn't, request to know who gave them the project. Ask them if other people were involved in

passing on the project. Finally, ask them who the original initiator was.

3. Find the people identified in the previous step and ask them the same questions.

4. If possible, confirm from the written records the original initiator's identity. This can be done through minutes of meetings, written correspondence, and reports.

5. Talk to other stakeholders and supporters of the project. The people who will be affected by the project may have a clue as to the identity of the project originator.

Identifying project beneficiaries

There are some people who will end up benefitting from the project even though they did not initiate the idea. Such people may have discussed their needs or interests during meetings or random conversations, with those needs being addressed by the project. These beneficiaries also need to be identified so that you get a clearer picture of what their specific interests are and how your project can meet their needs. Keep in mind that some of the people in this category may be totally unaware of the existence of your project, while some may be aware but don't know it can benefit them.

At the same time, identify any people who may not support the project. Determine their reasons for opposing the project and see how you can address their concerns. It could be that they do not have enough information about how they can benefit from the project, so take the time to explain this to them. In case they refuse to support the project, simply record their opposition as part of your risk-management plan.

Identifying the project champion

A project champion is someone who has authority and power within an organization and is willing to be a strong supporter of your project. They are ready to back you in disputes and meetings, and they do everything they can to make sure that your project succeeds. The mere fact that everyone knows this individual is a strong supporter of your project makes people recognize its significance and motivates them to work harder toward its success.

It is important that you identify someone within the organization who can play this role. If your project doesn't have a project champion already, recruit one. Talk to them about how this specific project will benefit them and what kind of help you may require from them. You should try your best to gauge their level of enthusiasm for the project and determine how much assistance they are willing to offer you.

Identifying the implementers and users of project results

At the end of the project, there are particular predetermined results that are expected. These results can be in form of products or services. The reality is that in most cases, the person who assigns you the project to create a product or service will not even use them.

This means that you have to identify the real users of the results of the project so that you can understand their needs and expectations. Furthermore, you also need to know the opinions of the team that will implement the project. To do this effectively, you need to clearly explain to the users and implementers about the product or service being produced. In case they have any extra needs that can be incorporated into your project, you should consider addressing them.

Clarifying the actual expectations of the project drivers

Sometimes the needs of a project are not as obvious as you may think. When you are assigned to a project, you are told to produce particular outcomes. However, you aren't informed about the needs you are supposed to address. These needs that your project is expected to meet in order to claim that it is successful are known as project requirements.

When defining your project requirements, you must determine the hopes and expectations that your project is meant to address. You must also find ways to ascertain that what people are telling you are the actual needs that they have. It is possible that some people aren't willing to share their real thoughts or feelings, or maybe they simply cannot put them into words clearly.

Determining whether your project is able to address needs

The organization should provide resources for conducting a feasibility study to confirm that your project can successfully meet the needs of people. This will help you get enough relevant information to determine the chances of project success or failure.

Highlight the importance of your project to the organization

Whether your project succeeds or not depends on the level of importance your organization attaches to your project. An organization will usually divert its limited resources from projects of little importance to those considered more significant. The value that people attach to your project will be influenced by its expected benefits and whether people recognize those benefits.

In order to make people more aware of the benefits of your project to the organization, you should:

- Search for documents that reveal the fact that your project has the same priorities as the organization. Such documents include the organization's long-term plan, annual budget, capital appropriations plan, and Key Performance Indicators (KPIs).

- Use the justification page of your scope statement to emphasize how your project is linked to the priorities of the organization.

Organizations have limited resources and cannot afford to be spending them on projects that are perceived to be lacking any value. It is your responsibility as project manager to get people to realize how positive an impact your project can have on the organization. Get them to focus on the results that have value.

Getting Your Project Objectives Right

Stating your objectives in a clear manner is one of the best ways to ensure that you achieve them. Project objectives can be products, services, or the results of using these products or services. Your objectives must incorporate the following elements:

- **Statement** – This is a short description of the results you intend to achieve.

- **Measures** – These are the indicators that you will use to evaluate your results.

- **Specifications** – These are the specific details or values of every indicator that will define the success of your project.

It is important to make your objectives as specific and clear as possible. Some project managers try to play it safe by establishing vague objectives or a range of values that will give them some wiggle room when defining success. This is a recipe for confusion because you may assume that the lower value of your objective signifies success, but the upper management may consider the upper value as the true indicator of success in the project. This is why you need to make sure that the objectives you come up with are as specific as possible.

How to create specific project objectives

1. Describe every objective briefly. Avoid the urge to fill a whole page with just one objective as very few people are likely to read it. In case they do, the

objective is unlikely to be interpreted in a clear manner.

2. Keep the language simple. Avoid using technical words or acronyms that may be prevalent within your field or industry. Do not use specialized languages that other departments within the organization may not understand. This is likely to cause misunderstandings and confusion. Make your objectives easy to understand by using language that anyone can understand.

3. Develop SMART objectives.

- *Specific* – Your objectives should be clear, detailed, and definite.

- *Measurable* – Indicate the indicators or measures you will use to judge if your objectives have been achieved.

- *Aggressive* – Make sure that your objectives are challenging enough to motivate people to do their best – and then some.

- *Realistic* – The project team needs to believe that they can achieve the set objectives.

- *Time sensitive* – There must be a date by which the objectives must have been achieved.

4. Be able to control your objectives. The project team must feel that they can steer every objective to a successful conclusion. If the team members believe

that they have no control and cannot influence their success, the objectives will not be achieved.

5. Determine what all the objectives are. Specifying every objective will help you use the available time and resources well to work toward achieving them.

6. Make sure that project drivers and supporters come to an agreement on the objectives of your project. If these two parties agree on your objectives, you will have the confidence to achieve success in your project. You will also have people around you who are willing to do their best to make the project a success.

How to handle resistance to your objectives

There are times when people may not want to commit to objectives that have been specified in a clear manner because they feel that it would be difficult to achieve them. However, vague and generalized objectives will make it much more difficult to recognize if the actual needs and expectations of the project drivers are being met. Simply put, it is highly likely that the project will fail if you do not have specific objectives.

There are several reasons that people may give to try to explain why specific objectives should not be established. These have been outlined below, together with the appropriate responses:

- **Specifying the project objectives will kill creativity:** While it is true that creativity should be nurtured within a project, there must be parameters for it. Specific objectives resolve the question of where creativity is allowed and when it should be used. Creativity can be used when determining how to meet the objectives of the project initiators/promoters, but the clearer these objectives are, the easier it will be to do so.

- **The project involves researching and then developing a new product/service, and it is impossible to know what will be accomplished:** Objectives are not meant to be guarantees. They are simply targets to reach for. Though there is the element of risk in projects that you have never done before, you must still state from the beginning precisely what you intend to achieve. It doesn't matter if you aren't sure if the task is possible, the length of time it will take, and the financial requirements involved. Set your specific objectives and modify them as the project progresses.

- **The needs or interests may change**: Nobody said that objectives should be set in stone. They are not the Ten Commandments. They are simply targets that rely on information that is available today. If things change in the future, then they will be assessed accordingly and changed if necessary.

- **The person requesting the project isn't sure what they want from the project**: Tell them to return when they know what they want the project to achieve. Otherwise, it would be a waste of resources if the project were to proceed and produce outcomes that would be rejected by the person.

Dealing with Project Constraints

Since we live in an imperfect world, you have to be realistic about your project. The expected results may not be achieved and the resources budgeted for may not be enough to complete the project. Welcome to the world of project constraints.

When you define your project constraints, you become more realistic about your plans and expectations. There are two types of constraints:

- Limitations – These are limits that are put on the project results, for example, the schedule, resources, and techniques to be used.

- Needs – These are project requirements that have to be met to achieve success.

These two types of constraints are reviewed in detail in the following sections.

How to identify your limitations

You must explore every source of information you have if you are to discover all the limitations in your project. There are certain methods that you can use, such as:

- Asking the project stakeholders. Consult the project promoters to determine results-based limitations. Talk to the project supporters to identify any limitation linked to performance and resources.

- Reading the organizational reports, plans, minutes, budgets, and reports of other similar projects.

When you find limitations to your project, note them down in your scope statement. These limitations will be very useful in the future when you need to know any alternatives that you can consider for your project plan.

Categories of limitations

Limitations must be identified early in the life of a project. For this reason, it is important to understand the categories that exist within a project setting. This will help you discover all the possible limitations that may affect your project. These categories include:

- **Results** – The project is expected to produce a product that must have a specific effect or feature. For example, the new product must cost less than $400 to develop.

- **Time** – The project is expected to be completed within a specific window of time.

- **Resources** – The project is only allowed to consume a set type and amount of resource.

- **The performance of activities** – The project activities can only be performed using particular strategies or techniques.

Always make sure that your limitations are clear and to the point. If the constraints aren't specified properly, it becomes difficult to determine whether you can meet their requirements and expectations. This will ultimately affect the successful completion of the project.

Chapter 4: Project Scheduling

Every project has deadlines. You may not be aware of the specific outcomes or results of your project, but there is an expectation that it will have to be completed sooner rather than later. However, no project manager is certain of when their project will be complete the moment they receive their assignment. This can be a scary experience because you don't have most of the facts yet and the project idea may even sound very complicated.

It is often assumed that costs are the most important thing when estimating and managing a project. However, the time element is of even greater importance. You must be able to set an accurate timeframe for project activities in order to meet goals successfully. You need to avoid the trap of setting too much time for the project, which may lead to people working slowly and not getting things done as fast as possible. There is also the trap of not allocating enough time, thus resulting in a rush job plagued by frustration and poor work quality.

Being able to accurately predict your project schedule is a

result of many years of experience and through trial and error. Managing your project time successfully is very important since it enables you to utilize the available resources and opportunities effectively. The longer a project continues the more financial resources it consumes. This is especially true when the project goes past its intended deadline.

Though every individual project has its own specific elements and will have a slightly different scheduling process, there are two aspects of time that you will have to manage. These are *planning the schedule* and *controlling the work*.

Planning the Schedule

This part of project schedule starts prior to the project taking off. The project manager and members of the project team come together and decompose the project into specific activities. Each activity is then allocated a specific duration of time. At this point of the planning process, you need to make sure that the team members who are helping you schedule the project have previous experience with the tasks and activities being defined.

Getting people with the required experience will benefit the project planning process immensely. Most of the work of scheduling tasks will involve decomposing the work packages down to their lowest levels. In other words, you are taking a large and general project activity and breaking it down into its smallest tasks. This is done through the Work Breakdown Structure. Once every work package has been identified, they must be arranged in a sequence in order to create a project schedule. You will also have to take into account any dependencies that link the project activities and tasks.

Finally, estimate the amount of time that every activity will require and develop your final project schedule. This will be a simple process if you have experts in your team who are experienced in those particular work activities. Now that you have planned your project schedule, the next step is to make sure that you control it.

Controlling the Work

There is a great need for a project manager to keep tabs on the project schedule to make sure it remains reasonable and accurate. In case there are particular tasks that are taking too long or being completed faster than was expected, adjust the overall schedule accordingly.

Every project schedule will face some sort of adjustment as work progresses. However, these changes will be easier to manage if they are made as early as possible. For this reason, you need to put in place a mechanism for accurate reporting. Create specific and predetermined checkpoints that will help you monitor the progress of team members as well as the project in general.

In order to effectively control your project schedule, you need to make use of specific documents to provide you with the necessary data. These are:

- Project calendars

- Schedule data

- Cultural and organizational guidelines

The key to tracking project progress and adjusting the work schedule is in precise and reliable reporting. As a project manager, you will need to get your team members to be part of this endeavor.

Reviewing the Process

As a project nears its completion, it is crucial that you take the opportunity to review not just the project activities but time management as well. This is not for the benefit of the current project but in order to learn lessons for any future projects.

You should examine the areas of the project that were completed faster than expected and those that took longer than planned. You will then have to ask yourself what measures can be taken to make sure that future projects are streamlined and completed faster.

It is easy to ignore this kind of review at the end of a project, primarily because everyone is thinking about winding up and moving on to something else. However, you need to practice the discipline of analyzing your successes and failure in time management so that you become a better project manager in the future.

How to Manage Your Project Schedule

Managing your project schedule means you have to take measures designed to ensure that your project is completed on time. You have to determine milestones and delivery dates as you also account for all the project constraints.

There are numerous risks and uncertainties associated with managing a project schedule. Therefore, make sure that the team members who will be doing the work are included in the process of planning the schedule. Giving them the opportunity to have some input will enable them to feel like they own the schedule. The estimates regarding the duration of activities and their sequence will also be more realistic.

Managing your project schedule will require you to plan the work and work the plan. This can be done by taking the following steps:

- Define your project activities – You need to break down the work packages into deliverables and tasks. This is then presented in the Work Breakdown Structure.

- Sequence your activities – Arrange the deliverable and tasks in an order that reflects how they will be done. Ensure that you account for any dependencies.

- Estimate the amount and types of resources needed – Your team must have a clear understanding of the availability and capacity of resources.

- Estimate the time necessary to complete each activity – This will help you determine your critical path and the total duration of the project.

- Develop the schedule – The accuracy of your schedule will depend on the sequence of activities, their timelines, and resource requirements. There is project management software that can help you simplify this step.

- Control the schedule – This step is the one that defines "working the plan" while the other previous ones represent "planning the work." It involves adjusting and modifying the project schedule as you see fit even as the project progresses.

The steps highlighted above are described in detail in the following section.

Defining Your Project Activities

The aim here is to identify the individual tasks in detail and estimate how much time and resources will be necessary to finish them. The input you will require at this stage is the scope baseline. The scope baseline is the starting point of breaking down the project deliverables. It guides the whole scope of the project so that activities do not stretch beyond what was agreed upon. It consists of the scope statement, the WBS, and the WBS dictionary. The WBS dictionary is simply a detailed and technical description of every element in the WBS.

In order to define every project activity, you will first have to take each work package and break it down into individual activities. A work package is the lowest level of the WBS. No single activity should be linked to two different work packages. Though every work package can be handled by a single team member, the activities under it can be shared out to several team members.

Here is an example:

Your Work Breakdown Structure may have the work package "Choose and Hire Subcontractor." This work package can be managed by one person. However, this work package can be split into different activities, each one being performed by a different team member. For example, Specifying task requirements; Identifying potential subcontractors; Sending invitations to tender, reviewing tenders, conducting interviews and finally appointing the subcontractor.

It is important to ensure that every activity under the work package is accurate and complete. The end result of breaking down a work package is an activity list that guides you in developing your project schedule. It is expected that every activity will have an assigned duration, but if this is not possible to do, then you should consider it to be a milestone instead.

When you have ultimately defined your activities, you will end up with an activity list, activity attributes, and a milestone list. Activity attributes describe the activity by highlighting its components, for example, the person responsible for undertaking the activity and the location of the work. A milestone is simply a significant point or event in a project. They can either be optional or contractual.

Sequencing Your Project Activities

After identifying your activities, you have to arrange them in the right order, making sure that you take into account their dependencies. A dependency is a link between two or more activities that must follow each other in sequence. For one activity to start, another activity must first be completed.

Classifying your dependencies is important because they act as indicators of the sequence that should be followed. There are four classes of dependencies. These are:

- Finish-to-start: This is where an activity must be completed before the next one begins.

- Start-to-start: This is where one activity can only start after another one has begun.

- Finish-to-finish: This is where an activity can only finish when another has finished.

- Start-to-finish: This is where an activity must begin before another is able to finish.

These dependencies can either be external (dependent on an entity outside the project e.g. suppliers) or internal (existing within the project). Once you have sequenced your project activities and factored in the dependencies, you end up with what is known as a *network diagram*.

Estimating Project Resources

Resources are the lifeline of any project. If every project activity is to be completed successfully, you will have to estimate the required resources. You do not have to worry too much about being accurate with your figures. An estimate can be reviewed at a later date.

There are several tools that you can use when trying to determine the resources your project activities will require. These are:

- **Expert judgment** – This can be provided by the

project team members, but in most cases, there is a need for outside expertise with the necessary skills and knowledge.

- **Alternative analysis** – This involves considering all the different options that you can use to assign resources. An activity can be accomplished in several ways. This means that you can vary the amount and type of resources depending on the technique of accomplishing the activity. This will then help you decide from the options available.

- **Published estimating data** – This involves utilizing data that has been published by other organizations. A project activity is compared to another similar activity whose estimates have been published. You use the closest comparable activity to the one you are trying to estimate. The weakness of this tool is that the organization that compiled and published the data may be very different to your own in terms of characteristics and resource capacity.

- **Project management software** – This is a set of computer-based tools that can help you develop your estimates for the resources required.

- **Bottom-up estimating** – The project activities are broken down further into component tasks. Individual estimates are then determined for every small task. The smaller task estimates are then added up to determine the larger activity estimate. The weakness of this tool is that it takes too much time, and sometimes it can be extremely difficult to break down activities that can't be defined easily.

Estimating the Time

In this step, you are required to estimate the effort necessary to perform a specific project activity and then calculate its duration. The effort is calculated by determining the work done during an activity. The time is calculated by dividing the effort by the estimated resources derived from step 3 above. You can use expert judgment based on information obtained from past projects that are similar in nature.

Developing the Schedule

This is the final step in the process, and by now you should have collected all the necessary information you need to develop the project schedule. This process can be done using scheduling tools that generate preliminary results. These results are based on:

- Predetermined activities

- Estimation of available resources

- Estimation of activity duration

- Dependencies

There are a number of tools that you can use to develop your project schedule. They include:

- Schedule network analysis

- Critical path method

- Schedule compression

- Critical chain method

- Resource leveling

- What-if scenario

Controlling the Schedule

In order to effectively control the schedule of your project, you will have to establish a schedule baseline. It is critical that you maintain this baseline so that the current status of progress can be monitored effectively.

When you control the schedule, you are:

- Determining the current state of the project

- Controlling those elements that may cause changes in the schedule

- Monitoring any changes in the schedule

- Handling any problems that the changes cause

There are several techniques that you can use to control the project schedule. Some of them include:

- Performance reviews

- Resource optimization techniques

- Modeling technique

- Project management software

The project schedule should never be underestimated. It is a significant part of your project and can make the difference between success and failure. Every project manager must have a schedule management plan in order to monitor any changes that occur and know how to manage them. This way, you will be able to ensure that project activities are executed as smoothly as possible.

Chapter 5: Managing Project Risks

One of the first things you have to do to ensure a successful project is come up with a plan that will help you generate the required project outcomes as per the schedule and budget. Some projects are relatively short, and these tend to be easier to plan for and complete successfully. However, there are some projects that are bigger, longer and more complex. These projects are likely to develop some unforeseen challenges that threaten to produce undesirable outcomes.

It is important to contemplate how you will deal with any potential risks that arise before and during a project. Risk management has to be part of your project plan. You must be able to identify and evaluate the impact that potential risks may have on the project, as well as any measures that need to be put in place to mitigate their consequences.

Risk Management

A risk can be defined as the probability of losing or gaining something of value. It is also the probability of not achieving project goals due to unforeseen internal or external vulnerabilities. Every project carries some inherent risks since it is very difficult to predict what will happen in the future. On the other hand, there are some elements that increase the risk of a project:

- The length of the project. Longer projects have greater risk.

- The time gap between project planning and project commencement. The bigger the gap, the greater the risk.

- New technology being used.

- Low level of experience of project manager or the team members.

Risks are not always negative in nature. They can sometimes be positive. Negative risks are also known as threats and have the potential to derail your project. Positive risks are also known as opportunities and have the potential of benefitting your project. A good example is where you decide to employ a smaller team than you originally intended.

Since the term risk is normally taken as something negative in project management, we shall examine risks from this particular viewpoint. The approaches and plans presented in this chapter are all associated with negative risk.

The process of identifying, assessing, and managing risks involve taking the steps outlined below:

1. **Risk identification** – Identify the aspects of your

project plan that may be vulnerable to changes.

2. **Evaluation of potential effects** – Think about the outcomes in case these aspects do not go according to plan.

3. **Development of mitigation measures** – Put in place plans that will minimize the consequences of these risks.

4. **Consistent tracking of project risks** - As the project progresses, assess whether the risks still exist, whether their probability of occurring is reducing or increasing, and whether there are any new risks coming up.

5. **Informing stakeholders of all potential risks** – Discuss with key audiences how the risks are likely to impact the project, from start to finish.

Risk Factors

Identifying your risks is the first step towards managing them. This is important because not all risks have the same impact on your project. The critical thing is to identify the ones that are most likely to affect your progress and success, and this means you have to identify the risk factors.

A risk factor can be defined as a situation that can lead to the occurrence of project risks. It is not the risk factor that causes a missed deadline. The risk factor simply increases the likelihood that another thing will happen to cause the missed deadline.

For example, you and your team may be undertaking a project that you do not have much experience in. The fact that you have never done such a project before may lead to an underestimation of the budget or time required. The lack of experience is considered a risk factor, but it is not what may lead to problems in the project. You may still succeed regardless of the low level of experience. However, it increases the likelihood that something else will happen to cause problems.

Risks must be managed throughout the life cycle of the project – from the starting to the close of the project. At every stage of the project, ensure that you have identified the risk factors. Some of the most common risk factors that affect all the stages of a project include:

- Failure to perform a formal feasibility study.

- Not getting approval for the project plan from all stakeholders.

- Failure by the project team to dedicate adequate time to one or more stages.

- Keeping poor records and reports, or failing to put important details in writing.

- Rushing through a stage and moving on to the next one without finishing all the required tasks.

- Not establishing any conflict resolution, decision making, or communication mechanisms.

- Transferring team members to other projects before closure of the current one.

Risk Identification

Every risk factor that you identify in your project will have its own specific risks. Once you have identified these individual risks, you will be in a better position to determine what the effects may be and how you will manage them.

So how do you find the risks associated with every risk factor you have identified? Follow these steps:

- Examine past project records to find problems that were encountered. You may discover that in a previous project similar to your current one, a risk factor actually caused an unanticipated risk. This information will help you prepare for the risks.

- Discuss with the relevant experts and stakeholders who have participated in such a project before. Use a lot of expert opinions to make sure that you have the best chance of identifying all possible risks.

- Describe the risk as specifically as possible. This will enable you to evaluate the potential effects.

Risk Evaluation

The probability of a risk occurring and its potential effects will determine the kind of consequences that should be expected. Once you are familiar with the expected consequences of the different risks, you need to decide which risks you want to deal with and which ones you can ignore.

In order to determine the likelihood of a risk occurring, you need to consider the following elements:

- **The chances that the risk will occur** – This may be expressed as a probability by using a scale of 0 to 1 or using percentages. In this format, 0 (or 0%) indicates that the risk is never going to happen, while 1 (or 100%) indicates that the risk is always going to happen.

- **Classifying the risks** – You can decide to use categories to help evaluate the chances of risks arising, for example, *always, often, sometimes,* or *never*. You can also use *high, medium,* or *low*.

- **Ordering the risks** – Create an ordered list where the first risk is the one that has the greatest probability of occurring, and the second risk has the next greatest probability, and so on.

- **Comparison of risk probability** – If you are assessing two risks, you can express the likelihood of occurrence by comparing their risk probability. For example, you can say that risk B is three times more likely to occur than risk A.

When evaluating the probability of risks occurring, you can rely on objective data from past similar projects if it exists. If this is the case, you should take a look at the past project records. It is recommended that you examine as many similar past projects as possible to increase the amount of objective information you can work with. The more similar the past projects are to your current one, the greater your confidence will be when it comes to making your conclusions.

Another way to evaluate the likelihood of risks is to use personal opinions. This is normally used in cases where there is little to no objective data records available. There may be people who have engaged in such projects in the past and are happy to share their opinions with you. You can interview them and ask them to rate the chances of potential risks occurring. You can use the categories described in the section above and then convert that data into a numbered scale. This will help you come up with a definitive weighted average of the probable risks.

If you want to get the best advice possible through personal opinions, you need to interview as many people as you can. Ensure that the projects they worked in are actually similar to your own. It is also recommended that the people you are interviewing do not share their opinions with each other before the interview. The opinions must be individual, not consensual.

Estimating the Consequences

Once you have managed to identify the probability of a risk occurring in your project, you will have to estimate the magnitude of the consequences. A risk with a big consequence should be treated differently from one that only presents lesser consequences.

In order to evaluate the consequences of specific risks, you will need to look at the impact on the entire project rather than just a section of it. The impact of a risk on may seem small if you assess it by its effects on intermediate milestones. However, if you consider the fact that the risk is going to affect the critical path of the project, you will see the bigger consequence emerge.

You also need to consider how related risks combine with each other to cause significant consequences. You can handle one task on the critical path experiencing a delay, but if you have three separate tasks on the critical path all experiencing delays, the magnitude of the risk becomes greater.

The Risk Management Strategy

Once you have evaluated your risks and the magnitude of their consequences, you need to develop a strategy for managing the potential negative effects. This risk-management strategy should guide you to determine whether to mitigate risks before they arise or as they occur. Such a perspective allows you to realize that mitigating the consequences of certain risks costs more time and effort than simply handling them when they arise.

There are a number of ways of handling those risks that you have decided to manage:

1. **Avoidance** – Take measures to neutralize the risk factor that caused the risk. For example, choosing to avoid using a new technology that may not yield the intended outcomes.

2. **Transfer** – Transfer the effects of the risk to a third

party and pay them for their services. A good example of this is buying insurance.

3. **Mitigation** – This can involve minimizing the chances of the risk occurring, or minimizing the negative effects in case the risk occurs. The first approach involves taking the necessary actions to prevent the unwanted situation from arising. The second approach is more about developing contingency measures to reduce the negative consequences of the risk after it happens.

There are also some very attractive, though unwise, ways of handling risks in a project. The approached described below are totally ineffective, so avoid them:

1. Denial – This is where you know that there is potential for a risk to arise but you simply refuse to accept that it may happen to you.

2. Praying – Waiting for God to fix all your problems or make them go away.

3. Ignoring – This is also known as the ostrich approach. You simply bury your head in your desk and ignore all the risks.

It is also important to communicate with your project team and relevant stakeholders about any risks that may threaten the success of the project. Do this in the early stages of the project as well as on regular occasions. Take the time to explain to people the nature of the risk, its impacts, and the methods you used to estimate its probability of occurrence. You also need to share the measures put in place to mitigate the risks.

Communicating the risks of a project with others can also be a way to prompt people to think and discuss the risks with the intention of reducing the unwanted consequences. Remember that all the information regarding the project risks must be documented in writing.

The Risk-Management Plan

This is a plan that describes the strategy to be used to reduce the negative consequences of uncertain situations. This plan should be developed during the organizing phase of the project. It should be constantly refined and updated as the project moves along. The components of the risk-management plan include:

- The risk factors identified

- The risks associated with individual risk factors

- How you assess the probability of each risk occurring and their consequences

- Mitigation and countermeasures

- How you intend to communicate with people about project risks throughout its life cycle

Chapter 6: Resource Management, Planning, and Budgeting

There is no disputing the fact that a project must have every available resource that it needs in order to be undertaken successfully. These resources can either be human or non-personnel. A project requires an investment in both of these classes of resources. Otherwise, the project will not be able to move forward as anticipated.

On top of the project plan and resources, a project must also be given the necessary funds to support its activities. In fact, every major decision affecting a project normally takes into account the project costs.

Resource Allocation and Management

Within a project setting, resources refer to the personnel, raw materials, equipment, tools, information, furniture, fixtures, and time. Most often than not, the resources that are available for a project can be somewhat limited. This means that there must be a tradeoff on what resources are allocated to project activities, how they are used, and when they are required. These are decisions that have to be made on a daily basis. That is why a resource allocation plan is necessary for the effective and efficient use of project resources.

There can be no effective management of resources without a resource plan to expound on the type of resource required and when it is needed. The timing of these needs also must be part of and align with the project schedule. In the event that the project schedule is changed, the resource plan should also be adjusted to align with the new changes.

Managing the unknowns

When developing a resource plan, it is highly unlikely that you will be in possession of every resource that is required for the project to take off. In most cases, the finer details of a project are rarely known at the beginning of the project. That is why it is very difficult to always know the type and scope of the resources needed.

When creating a project schedule, there will be those deliverables that can be broken down into individual tasks. However, there will also be other deliverables that cannot be broken down into sufficiently detailed tasks. If this is the case, then you should consider using a planning package.

A planning package is a component of the work breakdown structure. It contains a general description of the work that is to be done but does not clarify the detailed scheduled activities or the personnel to be assigned to these activities. Though it does not contain sufficient details, a planning package can still be used to define the specific scope of the project.

The details of the activities contained in a planning package are normally taken as known unknowns. In other words, the work has not been broken down into specific tasks. The individual resources, duration of tasks, and the personnel who will do the work have not been accurately described. You are essentially using reliable estimates based on industry standards or historical information.

There is nothing wrong with this approach. In fact, it is not necessary to break down all work activities and assign project team members to the tasks prior to starting the project. In most cases, the project manager establishes a baseline schedule and a resource plan using the estimates of a planning package.

Once the project begins and more information starts flowing in, the known unknowns become more explicit, and the necessary changes can then be made to the schedule and resource plan.

There are also some situations that are referred to as unknown unknowns. These are events that may possibly occur but cannot be planned for at all. An example is where a fire breaks out in the warehouse containing all the heavy equipment, thus resulting in project delay. This is something that no project manager can factor into their project plan. This is why it is best practice to update the resource management plan throughout the life of the project.

Resource Planning

How would you define a good resource plan? Such a plan must contain a detailed schedule of the work to be done, the kind of resources that each task will require, and the person who will be assigned to every task.

When assigning tasks to specific team members, you must know how long the task is expected to be performed, and the availability of necessary resources. You must also be aware of the skill set necessary to get the job done. This information is what guides a project manager as they analyze the project schedule, assuming that the required resources and skills are available.

The duration of individual tasks must be realistic. An activity may typically take, say, two weeks to complete. However, if you factor in general meetings and vacations that may hamper the availability of team members, it would be more reasonable to plan for a timeframe of three weeks.

There are generally two types of resource plans:

- **Hypothetical resource plan** – This is based on the assumption that the skills required for task completion are already available. It is a product of a hypothetical schedule.

- **Actual resource plan** – This is based on the definite availability of the resources required.

Assigning project work

As mentioned earlier, prior to the start of the project, the schedule and resource plan are created without consideration being given to the availability of resources. The next step after that is assigning work to team members.

At this stage, a project manager must use an element of psychology to ensure that he chooses the right person for the right task. Team members prefer being told in clear terms the work that they need to do, so make sure that you communicate well with them. In order to ensure that the work output is of the highest quality, there must be focused attention on the task at hand. Research has shown that multitasking more than three activities at the same time greatly hampers efficiency.

If you do not prioritize project tasks for your team members, they will likely opt to perform those tasks that they prefer doing, instead of the ones that are more critical to project progress and success. It is very important, therefore, that you get the team to understand where the priorities are so that the project plan is effectively executed.

Finally, you have to know how to handle schedule changes with regards to project assignments. Oftentimes, there are unforeseen adjustments to the project schedule, thus forcing the work assignments to also be modified. In order to achieve the best outcomes in such situations, you should consider handing out smaller, more frequent tasks to your team so as to create less confusion.

Resource Budgeting

A project budget refers to an estimate of all the resource costs in a project over a specific period of time. A budget normally evolves with time – starting with a draft estimate, morphing into a detailed estimate, and ending up as an approved budget. There are even some instances where you can update your approved budget as the project is ongoing.

As a project manager, you have to constantly make project decisions that ensure there is a good return on investment. There are a number of reasons why it is crucial to estimate the costs within a project:

- You are able to determine if the project is financially sensible by comparing the expected benefits and costs.

- You get the opportunity to see if the finances required to support the project are available.

- It helps give you the assurance that there are enough funds to finish the project.

Types of project costs
Project costs are divided into:

1. **Direct costs** – These are costs that can only be attributed to project resources. For example salaries for the project team, specific materials and equipment, work-related travel, and subcontracts.

2. **Indirect costs** – These are costs that cannot be directly attributed to one specific project. The costs can be for resources that span beyond just one project. For example, employee benefits, furniture, equipment, office rent, and general administrative costs (such as fees for legal and accounting services.

Stages of making a project budget

When an organization is making a decision about a project, the decision makers typically prefer to have a detailed and precise budget available so that they have the opportunity to evaluate the benefits of the proposed project and determine if there are adequate funds to finance it. The problem is that there is no budget estimate available at that stage because you do not have enough information regarding the kind of work and resources the project will need.

The truth is that such decisions to proceed with a project and how to go about doing so must be made prior to the preparation of detailed and precise budgets. In order for a budget to be inclusive of the fine details necessary for the support of critical project decisions, it needs to go through certain stages of development. These stages are meant to refine the project further and provide more accurate information:

1. Rough estimate

During this stage of budget making, an initial estimate is drawn up based on a general assessment of what the project will actually involve. It does not contain any detailed information, and the final approved budget may even end up being twice as big as this rough estimate.

A rough estimate can be prepared by researching the costs of similar projects undertaken in the past. You should also consider other factors such as applicable cost, productivity ratios, and methods of approximation.

A rough estimate only tells you what the project budget should be rather than what it actually will be. At this stage, you do not have the details regarding which specific tasks and activities the project will involve. You also do not have enough time to put the information required for a rough estimate together. That is why a rough estimate does not factor in too many details.

The reality is that majority of the budgets you see being presented as long-term plans or annual plans are simply rough estimates. These costs are subject to significant changes since the people responsible for making the estimate must continue to refine the budget as more details are received.

2. Detailed budget estimate

During this stage of the process, every project activity is identified and its corresponding cost is itemized. This is made possible by drawing up a Work Breakdown Structure (WBS) and using the lowest level of project activities to estimate the costs.

3. Complete and approved budget

This is the last stage of the budget making process. It is highly detailed and the decision makers examine it and agree to give it their backing.

How a budget evolves through the stages of a project

A project normally has four distinct stages: Starting, organizing and preparing, performing work activities and project closure. As your project goes through these four stages, your budget should also be refined and updated to include more relevant details. Your budget should evolve as follows:

1. When starting the project, create a rough estimate. This estimate is then used to consider the benefits and

costs of the project to the organization. Try to make sure that the costs that you specify in this rough estimate are as high as the project can go without compromising return on investment. At this stage, you cannot be confident in your budget estimate because it does not rely on any hard analysis of the project activities.

2. As you prepare and organize the project, you should also be refining your budget by adding more details. During this stage of the project, you have a clearer idea of what the project will entail in terms of work activities. Use this information to develop a detailed budget that will then be approved by the decision makers.

3. When the project is in the third stage (performing work activities), you will be able to identify the team members and project staff who will be part of the project. You will also have contractual agreements with vendors and suppliers for the use of facilities, equipment, or materials. All this information can now be added to the budget to make it more precise. This stage of the project usually sparks a lot of changes to be made to the budget, so you have to be alert to any changes that need to be made.

4. Once you have made changes to your project budget, you will have to seek approval again from the same people who approved the original budget. It is also recommended that you ask for permission to review the budget before you go ahead and do so.

5. In the closing stages of the project, you should

continue to track work activities and any changes that might necessitate a budgetary revision.

How to prepare a detailed budget estimate

If you have already prepared a rough estimate as your budget and are ready to organize and prepare your project, then you will need a detailed budget. There are two approaches to preparing a detailed budget estimate:

1. **The bottom-up approach** – This approach involves using the lowest-level work activity in the Work Breakdown Structure. All the lowest activities are assigned an estimated cost, and all these costs are then added up to determine the total project budget. Costs that you need to take into account for each activity include labor salaries, materials, equipment, travel, services, non-personnel resources, and indirect costs.

2. **The top-down approach** – This is where you settle on a total project budget first and then split that total cost among the lower levels of work activities in the Work Breakdown Structure. Keep in mind that you need to use a suitable ratio when you are dividing the total cost down to the lower levels. Ultimately, you will end up with a cost estimate for every work activity necessary for the project.

The important thing to remember is that a budget isn't really fixed. You can still refine it as you go along, making the required adjustments depending on project needs. Just make sure that you always seek approval before making any changes to the amounts that have already been approved.

Chapter 7: Picking the Right Project Team

What is the best way to go about picking the right project team? How do you go about organizing your project organization?

This is a very common question that every project manager needs to address as they plan their project. The people you bring into your team and assign tasks to must exhibit certain characteristics that will propel the project to eventual success.

Granted that there are different types of projects out there, the team you choose will depend on the specific kind of work you are engaged in. Since project conditions vary widely, there must be some general characteristics that any project manager can use to create a successful project team. Here are some ideas for picking the right project team.

The PAC Principle

As a project manager, you need to ensure that you have the right people working with you. So how do you know whether they fit into your team or not? You can use the PAC principle. PAC stands for:

- **Passion** - You want team members who are passionate about the project.

- **Ability** – Your team must have the required skills to do the job successfully.

- **Capacity** – Everyone on the team must have the time to do the job that is required.

The people you select as part of your team need to be interested in the problem/need that the project is supposed to solve. They should also show an interest in the technology that is being used to resolve the problem. Out of the three elements of the Pac principle, passion is the one that is likely o make the biggest difference in how the team works. If the team members do not like what they are doing, team morale will be low and work will not be done as effectively and efficiently as required. People will not use their abilities fully and this will lead to wastage of time and effort. The team must exhibit an intense desire for the tasks involved.

Your team members must have the skills necessary to get the job done. Every member of your tea must bring something to the table to contribute to the overall performance of the project. The last thing you need is to carry dead weight as you go along.

If you have already identified people who are passionate about the project and possess the necessary abilities for the job, ensure that they have time to do the job. A lot of times people assume that multitasking is a good thing since you are handling many different projects at the same time. This is normally touted as being productive. However, the truth is that trying to focus on several things at once leads to wastage of time, and ultimately, very little work gets done. Passion and ability may be present in the team, but if people cannot commit the required time to work on a project, they will still be ineffective.

The Generalizing Specialist

Once you have assembled a team that conforms to the PAC principle, the next step is to ensure that all the required skill sets are represented. For example, if you have a software development team, you would need skill sets such as developers, business analysts, DBAs, testers, technical writers, data modelers, designers, and e.t.c.

These are all specialists who will contribute immensely to your project team since every skill set will be represented. However, you need to consider what would happen if your team is too reliant on a particular individual to provide all the expertise on a specific skill set. In other words, how reliant is your team on the knowledge possessed by only a single person?

Another problem with having a team full of specialists is that there are times when a group of people will be working while the rest, who don't have those skills, will be sitting idle. This will cause a negative capacity balance.

Finally, having too many specialists creates a workflow process challenge. One person starts a task and maximizes on their skill. They then hand it off to the next person to work on since they don't have the skills to do the next part. This results in the need for extra documentation and records. It also leads people to adopt an attitude where a team member washes their hands once they are done with a task and doesn't really care about what happens after that.

The way to avoid such challenges is to make sure that your team has generalizing specialists. These are individuals who are a jack-of-all-trades. They possess some specialized skills in a few areas but they are also competent in other areas as well. The best thing for a project team is to have generalizing specialists who possess all the skills the project requires.

If your team is made up of generalizing specialists, they can teach others to improve their competency in those specific areas. The team becomes more rounded because if one person is not around, another seamlessly steps in to take their place. There will be less handing off of work since one person has the skills to perform a task from start to finish. The best thing about this is that your team will be very innovative and perform at a high level since people are willing and able to learn from each other.

Team Chemistry

Your team chemistry is a good way to know how effective it will be in performing its tasks. Once you have a team that has PAC and is full of generalizing specialists, you still need to make sure that the members can get along and work together. There are three characteristics of a team that has great chemistry:

- **Reflective Improvement** – The team is always seeking new ways to improve their ability to achieve project goals.

- **Osmotic Communication** – The team members are able to talk to each other in a natural way such that they can almost finish each other's sentences.

- **Personal Safety** – The team members are not afraid to speak honestly with each other. They are comfortable enough to suggest unconventional ideas since the environment is one of respect and trust.

If your team exhibits these characteristics, then you will have no problems getting them to work together with synergy. As a project manager, you have to take your time and effort to go through the journey of assembling a project team that will deliver successful results.

Qualities of a Project Team Member

There are certain qualities that every team member in a project should have. These are:

- **Effective communication skills** – A project team is comprised of different individuals coming from diverse backgrounds. Yet these people are supposed to communicate and work together to achieve project goals. This can only be possible if the team members develop the ability to communicate effectively with diverse audiences. Information must be relayed in a way that the people concerned understand. This is essential for project success.

- **High levels of organization** – Every team member must exhibit a high level of organization. There is no place for chaos and confusion in a project. No matter how stressful the environment may get, individuals must be able to use the tools and techniques available to handle the job.

- **An understanding of project management fundamentals** – This doesn't mean that everyone must be an expert in every PM technique or tool. It is important that every team member have working knowledge of project management principles so that they have a solid foundation to stand on.

- **A knack for reading people** – Being able to read people is a gift that makes team members able to motivate each other. Every team member is a leader in some way and must be able to develop a vision that inspires stakeholders and colleagues. When morale dips, they should know exactly what to do or say to get people motivated.

- **Be confident** – There are times when stakeholders within the organization may oppose some of the aspects of a project. A team member must be self-assured enough to be firm and politely resist such pressure. The needs and interests of the project must be protected when others try to put obstacles in the path.

Though many employees have some kind of suitable foundation required to be project team members, it is very important to train them in project management skills. This will enable them to hone the qualities described above.

Chapter 8: Defining Roles and Responsibilities

A project team is normally made up of people with diverse working styles and skill sets. In most cases, you will be working with people whom you have never worked with before. With the hectic schedule and limited resources available, a project manager must ensure that the team works well together to minimize errors and wastage while maximizing individual contributions. Everyone on the team must have a clear understanding of what role they play and their corresponding responsibilities.

Understanding Project Roles

Every project involves activities such as performing particular tasks, making decisions and directing the activities of subordinates. Work must be done in a specific sequence and at maximum efficiency, making sure that people don't duplicate the work already done by others.

In order to clarify how the project team should relate to one another and to their assignments, it is important to first distinguish three specific roles that individuals play within the team. These are:

- **Authority** – This is the capability to make binding decisions regarding a project's resources, schedule, products, and activities. For example, you may only be given the authority to make purchases that are less than $4000.

- **Responsibility** – This is the commitment that a person makes to achieve a particular result. For example, your commitment to preparing and presenting a report by a specific date.

- **Accountability** – Accepting the consequences in response to the performance. For example, your Departmental Manager noting in your performance appraisal report that you surpassed the set targets. Most people associate accountability with something negative, even though it also has a positive aspect in terms of being rewarded.

Most people tend to get confused when asked to distinguish between the three terms above. Though related, the terms are different and necessary when defining the roles of team members.

Prior to starting a project, it is imperative that there be an upfront agreement as to who will be making which decisions and who will be tasked with achieving particular results. This is where the difference between authority and responsibility comes in. Authority looks at the processes. It defines the decisions that need to be made with no focus whatsoever on the results that need to be achieved. Responsibility, on the other hand, looks at the outcomes. It deals with the results that must be achieved with no focus whatsoever on the decisions that are made to achieve these results.

One thing that every project manager needs to note is that you can delegate authority to someone else but you cannot delegate responsibility. If you give a team member the authority to sign off on certain decisions while you are away, and they end up making mistakes, you as the project manager will still bear responsibility. Authority can be taken back but you cannot blame the person whom you transferred the authority to.

Handling Project Assignments

In order to make a project a success, you have to rope in the talents of your project team members. This involves the delegation of roles, sharing out responsibilities, and making sure that there is total accountability.

Delegation

Delegation, in its simplest terms, refers to taking something that you have and giving it away. So would a project manager choose to delegate their authority?

- To create more time to perform other assignments

- To maximize on the decision-making skills of a qualified team member

- To get fresh ideas from another qualified team

member

- To train a team member and improve their capacity to handle extra workload successfully

Delegating certain tasks can help a project manager be more effective at his job. However, not all tasks can or should be delegated. The following criteria should guide you to know how to delegate project tasks:

- Don't delegate tasks that you are the best at – If you are the best person to perform a particular task, do not assign it to someone else. Do it yourself and assign someone else to do tasks that you aren't very skilled at.

- If possible, avoid taking on tasks that are on the critical path of the project. If any task on the critical path of a project is delayed, the project's estimated end date may have to be postponed. A project manager is constantly getting involved in different tasks. If they take on a critical-path task and are then called to resolve a problem in another task, delays will result.

- Do not delegate tasks that you are unable to describe clearly – If you find it difficult to clearly describe a particular task, do not give it to someone else. They will be constantly checking in with you to clarify certain issues, which is a waste of time. Just handle it yourself if you can.

How to delegate to achieve results

There are some steps that a project manager can take to make sure that the person they have delegated authority to succeeds in their assignment:

1. Be clear about the tasks that you have delegated and the expected results. If you feel it is necessary, also explain what you do not want them to do.

2. Pick the right person for the job. Before you choose someone to delegate authority to, determine the skills and experience level you require for the role. Do not give away authority to someone who does not possess these qualities.

3. Delegate the assignment in an appropriate and professional manner. Explain to the person what needs to be done, the effort you expect to be put into the task, and the deadline for the task. Ensure that you have all this noted down for future reference.

4. Maintain contact with the person you have delegated to so that you can resolve any issues or questions as they arise. This will also give the impression that you are actually concerned with the task.

5. Keep track of the person's performance. Make sure that you check in at regular intervals to monitor performance.

6. Be quick to resolve any problems that crop up. In case the person isn't performing the task as desired, talk to them and strategize on how to bring it back on track.

Micromanagement

Micromanagement is defined as the extreme, improper, and needless involvement in a task that you have already delegated to someone else. If one of the managers adopts this kind of approach with the project team members, there will be wastage of time and energy, not to mention poor motivation and tension.

Why would a manager micromanage tasks being performed by other team members? There are times when it is difficult to determine whether micromanagement is actually occurring. The subordinate may try to indicate in some way that the boss's oversight is a bit too much. If nothing changes, then it would be a good idea to try to figure out why the micromanagement is happening. There may be a number of reasons for it, namely:

- The micromanager is enthusiastic about the task. The best way to handle this would be to schedule specific times to talk about the parts of the task that they find interesting. This way, they do not bother you while working.

- The micromanager has great technical skills in the area and feels that they are better suited to perform the task. The solution is to frequently review the work with them so that they have chances to give their technical input.

- The micromanager may feel that the task was not explained clearly or they may fear that something might go wrong. The way around this is to create specific times and intervals for reviewing the work with the manager so that they are able to detect any errors and help you fix them.

- The micromanager wants to keep tabs on the assignment and maintain some involvement with the person. The solution is to send them regularly scheduled reports regarding progress. You should also consider dropping by their office regularly just to greet them.

- The micromanager fears that the person given the task has more technical skills than them. This should be handled tactfully by giving the manager credit whenever you discuss the task in front of other team members. You can also regularly share some of the pertinent details of the assignment.

- The micromanager wants to stay up-to-date with what is happening in the project in case their superior asks about it. This can be resolved by agreeing to the kind of information they need and how frequently it is required. Agree on a timetable for providing the relevant progress reports.

How to gain the trust of a micromanager

It is possible that the person doing the micromanaging is behaving that way because they don't fully trust in your ability to get the job done. It is easy to fall into the trap of feeling resentful and angry, but there's a better way to get them to have greater confidence in you. The steps below highlight how to deal with such a situation:

- Do not become angry, resentful, or defensive when

they ask you questions. If you behave like this, it sends the signal that you are not being totally transparent, thus increasing their mistrust of you. Just answer their questions and give them the details that they want.

- Let the manager know that you appreciate their interest, time, and input. If you are always grumbling about how their oversight is excessive, the relationship will become tense and they will find it even more difficult to trust you. First, thank them for their guidance and then try to build a better working relationship for the two of you.

- Suggest to the manager that you take the time to explain your approach to the tasks at hand. When they discover just how appropriate and advanced your working methods are, they will feel more confident in your abilities.

- Collaborate with the manager from the outset on how to create checkpoints where they are able to track your progress. This will give them the reassurance they seek.

Dealing with a micromanager requires patience and tact. If you follow the guidelines highlighted above, you will be able to gain their trust and create a better working relationship with them.

Chapter 9: Evaluating Project Results

Project evaluation can be defined as the systematic and objective assessment of a project that is in progress or already complete. The goal of evaluating a project is to establish to what extent the objectives have been achieved and how relevant they are. It is also a way to determine the efficiency, effectiveness, sustainability, and impact of a project. The evaluation process also enables the stakeholders to learn lessons from the project and thus make better decisions.

There are generally three types of project evaluations:

1. Pre-project evaluation

2. Ongoing evaluation

3. Post-project evaluation

The general perspective is that the ongoing evaluation is the most important of the three types of evaluations. The reason for this is that it provides the project manager with the ability to right the ship in case it is headed for the rocks. An ongoing evaluation will enable you to check whether your planning, organizing, directing, staffing, and controlling functions are being accomplished effectively. Since a project can be described as an organization with a highly decentralized structure, this type of evaluation is the most accurate and definite way to determine how effective the project is and its ultimate success.

As a project manager, the evaluation process requires that you exercise judgment based on the best information available at that particular time. The data that you use for measurement purposes during your evaluation must be factual. Don't forget that this process also requires the input of your project team when making the necessary decisions.

This chapter will specifically cover strategies used for an ongoing evaluation, as well as other areas related to this type of evaluation.

Ongoing Project Evaluation

When you decide to evaluate your project as it goes on, you are essentially engaging in the control function of project management. You are making sure that the resources that were availed for your project are being utilized effectively, and the project is proceeding on schedule, within budget, and as per technical requirements.

Every control system that is used in a project must include four key aspects:

- Performance standards generated from goals,

objectives, and strategies

- Techniques for measuring performance

- Comparison of actual and planned performance

- Corrective measures

It is critical that an ongoing project evaluation continuously searches for feedback on project progress. The following are specific questions that you can ask when trying to find information about the status of your project:

- What is right in the project?

- Are there any aspects, areas or elements of the project that aren't going the right way?

- Are there any emerging problems?

- Are there any emerging opportunities?

- Is the project on schedule, within budget, and meeting the technical performance standards?

- Is the project still aligned with the organization's strategic mission?

- Are there any additional actions that can be taken?

- Are the project results acceptable to the stakeholders?

- Are the customers satisfied with how the project is proceeding?

These are the types of questions that you can use during your regular project review meetings so as to encourage team members to think and discuss project issues. Therefore, your evaluation process will be effective and complete.

Measuring your Project's Results

When evaluating a project, the project manager is typically in one of two situations; either they have information, or they don't have it but know where to find it. In most cases, the project manager is overwhelmed by a lot of project data yet they are unable to find any relevant information that can help them determine the status of their project.

In order to measure project results, you must be guided by the following philosophies:

1. The aim is to measure project results and trends using information derived from the project Work Breakdown Structure.

2. The performance measurements obtained must be guided by the judgment of the experts conducting the evaluation.

3. Measurements must be taken around critical result areas that were already planned.

4. Measurements developed must be suitable for use both in the current results as well as future projections.

5. There should be integration of work package

measurements into the project as a whole.

There are certain key areas of a project that must be considered as "directional indicators." These are the areas that will guide you when you are seeking information on project progress, effectiveness, and efficiency. They include:

- Schedule parameters

- Cost parameters

- Financial returns

- Technical performance parameters

- Productivity

- Alignment with organizational strategies

- Competitiveness

It is the organization's strategic plan that contains these key result areas. It is therefore extremely important that these key areas be developed early on in the project, primarily during the pre-project evaluation phase.

It is important to note that in today's project environment, project managers are increasingly being held accountable by a multitude of stakeholders, with every stakeholder feels that their input is worthy. It is therefore extremely important that you remain cognizant of the need to continuously evaluate your project to know where it is going. You and your project team must remember that as the project is being evaluated, your performance is also being evaluated.

Chapter 10: Reporting Project Status

Reporting on the status of your project is a key function that you are expected to perform on a regular basis. Upper management and the project team may want to know how far the project has gone and the results that have been produced so far. The reality is that majority of project managers do not clearly understand how to report their project results. This is true even for the expert managers.

The cause of this is the issue of perspective. Most people have very little understanding of the perspective that they are supposed to have when approaching such a task. The senior manager who requests a project status report wants certain kinds of information included in the report so that they can present it to their boss. If you prepare a report that fails to have your manager's perspective, you might as well have not wasted your time at all.

There are some basic principles that you can use when reporting on the status of your project. These principles will help you keep all the stakeholders informed about project results and thus drive your project to success.

The Management Perspective

Your superiors are always interested to know the status of your project. They want to know how the resources that were availed to you have been utilized. This will be more so if your project is considered by the organization to be an important project. By preparing and presenting a proper status report, your managers will get a better picture of the health and general direction of your project. Your boss does not want to have to come down to the work site to find out what is going on. Remember that your boss also has a boss who is holding them accountable, so the information that you present must show that they too are in control of the project.

Excellent reporting on project status creates clarity from confusion. It is your responsibility as the project manager to collect all the available data, sift through it to get the relevant information required, and then condense it down into the most critical elements. You are expected to condense the results of thousands of work hours into information that your manager can read through and understand within five minutes.

There are three things that you have to keep in mind when reporting on the status of your project. These are:

- The three project status components

- Summarizing the details

- Critical data required by management

Project Status Components

The three primary components of reporting project status are:

- **Overall** – This represents the overall health of the project. Supervising managers need to have information that will help them determine if a project is in trouble. As a project manager, you may think that your project is in good health, but the supervising managers may have additional information that you do not.

- **Milestones** – There are major project activities that must be completed by certain dates. A supervising manager wants to see how many milestones have been completed, how many are still unfinished, and the ones that are coming up in the near future. This gives them the opportunity to evaluate the project schedule and make the necessary decisions.

- **Issues** – There could be some challenges or obstacles that your project may be facing. These issues could prevent your project from being completed successfully. A supervising manager would like to get a summary of every challenge or obstacle so that they can decide whether to let you handle it or step in and help.

How to Organize your Project Status Report

When presenting your project results, you need to arrange it according to priority. The overall health of the project should be first. If the supervising manager is pleased with that part, they may not even read the rest of the status report. The major milestones should then follow. In case the health of the project is not satisfactory, the supervisor will look at the scheduled dates coming up and how work is progressing toward them. If there are problems with the way milestones are being achieved, the next section should provide reasons why. This final section contains the issues that may be hindering the achievement of milestones. Make sure that the most pressing or impactful issue is presented first.

Summarizing your details

Another thing to remember is that the details in your report need to be summarized. Your supervisor does not have a whole half hour to spend thumbing through pages of information and project statistics. They are normally very busy overseeing many other projects so the most they can afford at times is 60 seconds.

While it may seem detrimental to you as project manager to keep the details brief, your supervisor does not see it that way. Maybe you want to show off how much you have achieved. However, it is important that you learn how to write a project status report without being long-winded. The following steps may help you:

- Present your information in bullet form, not prose. Avoid the use of paragraphs.

- Do not use titles extravagantly. Keep things simple and clear.'

- Summarize and shorten your sentences and expressions.

- Try not to use too many adjectives (bad, terrible, great) and adverbs (very, too, really).

Key Data

Even as you prioritize and summarize your project report, make sure that you always include key data. This will enable the supervising manager to objectively consider the project's overall health, performance, and potential threats. Some of the key data to describe overall health include:

- The planned completion as a percentage

- The actual completion as a percentage

- How many days/weeks you are ahead or behind schedule

- The number of obstacles you are facing

Some of the key data related to your milestones include:

- Name of milestone

- Percentage completion of milestones

- Planned start date of milestones

- Actual start date of milestones

- Planned completion date of milestones

- Actual completion date of milestones

The status of the overall health of a project is usually color-coded using red, yellow, or green. It is not really necessary to do the same for the milestones.

Issue Management

Listing the main issues or threats that you face in your project forms the final part of the project status report. The critical data that you have to include here is:

- Name of the issue – Try to describe the issue briefly.

- Time and date it was reported – If an issue has been pending for a long time, then someone must be held accountable.

- The severity of the issue – Is it an issue that blocks project progress and is likely to compromise the completion date? Is it a small problem that can be fixed quickly and isn't a big threat to the project?

- The person responsible for sorting out the issue

- ETA – Clarify when the issue will be resolved. Give a time and date if possible. If you cannot, then specify when the next phase of the issue resolution will be.

- Current action – What action is being taken to mitigate the issue? What alternatives do you have to the current actions?

You should try as often as possible to submit your project

status report to management. Do not wait to receive a request for a report. As a project manager, you want management to have confidence in your abilities and trust you to run the project the best way you see fit.

However, after they read the status report, they may decide to intervene and help you out if the overall health isn't good. Either of the two results – passivity or active intervention – is better than not sending a status report. Make sure that your report is always sent on a regular basis and to the right people.

Chapter 11: Closing the Project

One of the main characteristics of a project is that it has a defined end date. This is the date when it is expected that project activities will have been completed and objectives achieved. In most cases, however, the project manager comes under pressure to move on to the next project as quickly as possible, thus leading to a lack of closure for project participants.

Why is it important to bring a project to closure? The process of closing a project ensures that everyone is able to assess the extent to which the project achieved its intended goals. It allows you to know just how well you planned and executed the project. Furthermore, the team members are able to evaluate what they have achieved and celebrate accordingly.

Regardless of whether the project is a small or large, project closure is very important. Even if the team is moving on to another phase of a large project, it is still important to make sure that the previous phase has closure.

There are usually several minor details and pending issues

that are linked to closing a project. These issues may appear small but they have the tendency of piling up on you and frustrating your efforts. There are certain conditions that can make project closure harder than it should be:

- Lack of a written list of the activities that must be performed during project closure.

- Transfer of some team members to other projects midway through a project, thus forcing the others to take on extra responsibilities.

- Loss of motivation and interest towards the end of the project as team members shift their focus to new projects.

- Delays by the project staff who want the project to go on because they don't want to move on to other assignments or have become attached to their colleagues.

- The project customers are disinterested in finalizing the details of the project.

The best way to prevent such scenarios from occurring is to plan how you will undertake the closing part of your overall project plan. You should also identify the details that may cause problems and resolve them early, as well as refocus the energies of your team.

Planning For Closure

If you want to have a successful project closure, then you

should start thinking in detail about it as you prepare your project plan prior to commencing the project. Here are some of the things you must do when planning for project closure:

- Create a checklist of the things that must be done during closure of the project. Specify who will do them, when they will be done, and the resources they will require. For example, all incomplete activities and deliverables must be completed. The necessary approvals of project results must be obtained. There are administrative tasks that need to be performed. All contracts linked to the provision of goods and services must be terminated. It is also important to evaluate the extent to which expectations were met. The list should also consider how and where team members will be transitioned, as well as the location for storage of project documentation and deliverables.

- Add the closure tasks in the project plan. Every project has a work breakdown structure (WBS). This document should include activities that must be performed during project closure so that there are adequate resources and time allocated to them.

As the project winds down, you should encourage your team to view the closing phase as a separate task containing its own objectives, activities, and resources. This would also be a good time to take a closer look at the closure plans specified in the project plan. In case you need to update them, please do so.

In most projects that are in their final stages, it is common to find that team members start to focus on their own individual assignments rather than the collective ones. Other key stakeholders may also start to lose interest in the project and its results. As the project manager, you should make sure that commitment to project goals and enthusiasm for success does not go down. Every participant needs to play their part even as the project nears completion. In order to maintain focus and motivation, consider doing the following:

- Take the time to remind team members of the benefits that will be obtained from the final results of the project. Tell them that these benefits will be organizational as well as individual. This will trigger them to put in more effort to finish the project knowing that there are benefits that will be accrued.

- Gather your team together and remind them of your total commitment to making the project a success. Let them know the reasons why the project is important and encourage them to keep their eyes focused on the finish line.

- Create intermediate milestones and track the progress of your closure activities. Stay in touch with each team member and comment on their performance and progress as you wind up. This will enable you to know the extent of closure activities, while also providing them with information regarding the same. If there are any problems or issues that individuals have, then you will be able to find out and deal with them.

- Make sure that every team member can reach you. This is a crucial time in the project and your presence and voice may be required to reassure and motivate team members. By staying accessible, you send the message that you are still focused on the project and consider the work they do to be critical.

Dealing with Administrative Issues

When a project begins, team members are given the authority to spend money and time on activities associated with the project. As the project concludes, you should start to cancel such authorization so that people do not continue to utilize resources, especially on tasks that are no longer necessary.

The terminating process may involve getting all the necessary approvals from the client. This is to ensure that the project has met all the required standards and therefore no more work needs to be done. Another administrative issue that needs to be dealt with is the reconciliation of all pending transactions. Pay all the outstanding bills, resolve any disputes with suppliers, and cancel any supply contracts that you no longer need.

Transitioning your team members

Most project staff begin to worry about their next assignments the moment they realize that the project is about to close. This may affect their ability to complete their remaining tasks successfully. You need to be able to handle their transition well and help them move on to their next assignments. Encourage the team to wind up their responsibilities and assure them about their next assignments so that they don't worry needlessly. In order to provide a decent transition, consider taking the following steps:

1. Ensure that every team member's contribution has been acknowledged and documented. Talk to your team collectively and individually, thanking them for their efforts during the project and sharing your assessment of their performance. If you borrowed some individuals from other departments, thank their supervisors and share your performance review with them. It is recommended that the collective feedback you give in public be positive. Only share your criticism and suggestions for improvement when you are talking to individuals in private. Either way, you should also make sure that you follow up your comments in writing.

2. Offer your professional assistance to team members who need help finding new projects. Help them develop a transition plan that contains a schedule of how they should finalize their current assignments and fulfill their responsibilities.

3. Inform the organization or stakeholders that the project is finished. This can be done in writing or verbally in a meeting. Announcing project closure informs people that the benefits they were expecting from the project are now available. It also provides confirmation to all stakeholders associated with the project that their efforts have borne fruit. Finally, it informs people that resources and time can no longer be charged to the project.

4. Share with all stakeholders how much of a positive impact they had on your project. Let them know how valuable their support and investment was to achieving the results. This will motivate them to want

to support the next project.

Post-Project Review

This is an evaluation of the activities, processes, and results of the project. It is a way of evaluating the lessons that you have learned from the project so that you will be able to mimic what went right and avoid the mistakes that were made. It is also referred to as a post-project evaluation.

Preparing for the post-project review involves evaluating what the situation was before the project was implemented and then comparing it to the outcomes of the completed project. It allows you to develop a framework for defining the success of your project and whether project objectives have been achieved.

As the project progresses, team members are encouraged to note down any problems they face as well as successes that they experienced. These comments should be recorded in a computer file and then reviewed during the post-project review meeting. It is also important to keep files related to costs, labor charges, and performance reviews. When the project closes, the stakeholders should be interviewed to find out their opinions on the project performance, as well how they feel it met their needs.

The Evaluation Meeting

In order to carry out a good post-project review, you will need to collect a wide range of information, such as:

- Project results

- Expenditure

- Performance

- Problems faced

- Lessons learned

- Changes that occurred during the project

The above information can be obtained from correspondence between stakeholders, schedule reports, progress reports, cost reports, project memos, project logs, minutes of meetings, and e.t.c.

For the actual meeting, make sure that everyone who contributed to the project is invited to attend. If there are too many people to have in one meeting, consider splitting the list into smaller groups and meeting with them separately. If possible, call a final meeting where everyone may attend and review the minutes of the smaller meetings.

It is important to note that the post-project review meeting should not be allowed to degenerate into an accusation session. It should be a time to learn and examine the successes and failures of the project process.

The meeting agenda should include:

- Whether the project objectives were achieved

- Whether the project was completed on time

- Whether the project was within budget

- The challenges and problems faced and whether they could have been mitigated

- The effectiveness and efficiency with which the problems were handled

Make sure that someone is appointed to take down notes of the meeting. The records should indicate the names of those who attended the meeting, the information that was discussed, lessons learned, corrective actions to be taken, and the people tasked with executing those actions.

Chapter 12: Project Management Challenges and Failures

Being a project manager requires you to be adept at balancing the many components that constitute a complex project. You have to know how to control your project schedule, costs, scope, and personnel. Acquiring such a skill requires training and years of experience. If a project manager is not able to step up and take control of the many variables and risks that occur during a project, the project may end in failure.

Top 10 Project Management Challenges

There are a number of challenges that may arise during a project. Here are ten of the most common challenges that a project manager may encounter:

1. Lack of defined goals
Failure to clearly define what the goals of the project are is a recipe for chaos and disaster. It will definitely be a headache for the project team and staff. It is critical for the success of

the project that the project goals are agreed upon by upper management and these goals be supported throughout the life cycle of the project. These goals must be identified from the outset so that the significance of the project is clear for all to see. It is the responsibility of the project manager to know the right questions to ask that will help in establishing and communicating clear goals.

2. Scope creep

Scope creep refers to sudden or unplanned increases in the scope of an ongoing project. Once the scope of a project has been agreed upon by all parties involved, it is never a good idea to suddenly expand it without proper consultation with all stakeholders. There are times when a project manager is under pressure from the client or project supervisor to extend the scope beyond its original objectives. The project manager then has to evaluate the request to determine how the change will impact the project. The budget may increase, the schedule may have to be extended, or extra resources may be required. Such changes pose a challenge to a project manager, and they have to communicate this to the stakeholders.

3. Inadequate skilled labor

There are some projects that require specialized personnel that may not be available. This is a challenge that affects the working of the project team. The project manager must be able to assess the project activities in relation to the needed competencies, and determine if the available personnel can do the job. If the project staff does not have the required skills, they can be sent out for further training. Alternatively, the project can outsource the specialized tasks or hire temporary skilled labor.

4. Lack of accountability

Nothing brings a project to a complete stop like a failure to be accountable for one's actions. This does not just apply to the project manager but to every individual who is participating in the project. Pointing fingers at each other and playing the blame game is unproductive. Sadly, it is very common in most projects to meet this particular challenge. If everyone can simply agree to take responsibility for their role, the project can be successful. It is important that a project manager learns how to get his team together and align them towards achieving a common goal.

5. Poor risk management

Part of the responsibility of a project manager is dealing with and planning for unintended undesirable outcomes. Very few projects ever go according to plan, so you have to be able to have a certain level of risk tolerance. You need to collect the relevant data, develop trust, and be familiar with the areas of the project that have the greatest probability of not going to plan.

6. Undefined contingency plans

There has to be a pre-determined plan that clarifies what is to be done in case things don't work out as planned. The contingency plan must be well thought out and be able to cover specific scenarios. A project manager who fails to create a clear contingency plan may experience unexpected problems that stall the project. You can also use ideas from your project team and other stakeholders to identify areas where problems may potentially arise.

7. Poor communication

A lack of effective communication between project team members is one of the first signs of a project that is headed for failure. It is the job of the project manager to make sure that the communication strategy is well defined before the project begins. Every team member must be made aware of how the team will be communicating. The project manager must ensure that all team members know what is happening so that there is synergy. Communication can be written or oral, and feedback must flow from top to bottom and vice versa.

8. Unreasonable deadlines
There are times when a project faces tight deadlines. However, if a project manager is constantly asking his team to deliver impossible deadlines, low morale, and reduced productivity will plague the project. It is not feasible to expect team members to consistently work under deadlines that are unreasonable.

9. Insufficient resources
One of the main characteristics of a project is it requires resources. If these resources are not adequate, project activities will not be undertaken as effectively and efficiently as they should be. Resource deprivation is a serious challenge for a project manager to face. That is why it is crucial for the project needs to be defined and approved from the outset. The available resources must also be assigned and prioritized accordingly throughout the project.

10. Poor stakeholder engagement
If stakeholders do not engage with each other as required, the project will suffer. It can be one team member who is slacking off or a CEO who is not showing interest in the project activities. The project manager has to step up and ensure that there exists open engagement and feedback every step of the way.

Ten Major Causes of Project Failure

Most project managers are aware of the tips, guidelines, and resources that can help them make a project a success. However, project failure is one side of the coin that nobody wants to talk about. It's obvious why this is such a touchy topic for most people in management.

Failure is one of the harsh realities of life, but refusing to tackle it does not make it go away. In this section, you will learn about ten of the biggest causes of failure in projects. Hopefully, this knowledge will help you be better prepared for your next project management job:

1. Lack of adequate preparation

You must have a clear vision of what needs to be achieved before the project begins. This is essential for preparing for a project. If you do not prepare for your project adequately, you will not be able to get the team to focus on the end goal. How will you even know what project success looks like? It is critical that all stakeholders sit down during the project planning phase and agree on what their expectations are regarding the schedule, budget, and quality.

2. Poor leadership

A project has many leaders at different levels, so leadership does not just refer to the project manager. Every leader at every management level needs to take seriously their responsibility in making sure that success is achieved. Upper management should also show good leadership by supporting the project manager.

3. Lack of proper documentation and monitoring

The project manager must make sure that project documents and records are in good order at all times. Your records are what you and other stakeholders will use to determine whether the project is heading in the right direction. By having proper documentation and monitoring milestones, you will be able to allocate resources where they are needed the most.

4. Poor communication

This is one of the challenges mentioned in the preceding section and it is clear why it is a major factor in project failure. When people within the project organization do not communicate effectively with each other, it becomes very difficult to have focus and unity that drive the team forward. Communication failures can occur between the upper level of management, mid-level, or the project team. People should not feel afraid to step forward and speak their mind regarding the project. It is important for everyone to be open and transparent so that people understand one another and move forward as a unit.

5. Failure to define and enforce work standards

As a project manager, you are in charge of establishing the required standards for every task and goal. If there are team members who are not adhering to those set parameters, then you have to take the necessary action. Enforcing these parameters requires that you have a good working relationship with your team. Make sure that you give out assignments based on priority and to the most proficient individuals.

6. Failure to estimate costs accurately

You may find that some of the cost estimates you had are completely wrong. Every project requires adequate resources to run smoothly, and there are no exceptions to this rule. If the money runs out, the project stalls. This can be avoided by making sure that lack of resources is identified early so that measures can be put in place to resolve the situation.

7. Lack of experience

A project manager has to be able to juggle many different responsibilities. It is important for the manager to be given responsibilities that match their experience and education. Inexperience does not have to mean you have never managed a project before. It could mean that the role you are playing is at a higher level than what you are used to. If this is the case, it is possible for a project manager to be overwhelmed by their responsibilities, thus leading to failure to achieve project goals. While it is good to take on bigger challenges, just make sure that you do not bite off more than you can chew.

8. Competing priorities

A project may experience competing priorities in cases where there are inadequate resources to go around. This is why the project manager must ensure that budget cost estimates are as accurate as possible.

9. Wrong organizational culture or ethics

A project organization should be built on the foundation of competence, professionalism and pro-activeness. This kind of culture will motivate the team members to work hard and invest time and effort in making the project a success.

10. Ignoring warning signs

No project fails abruptly. Before a project fails, there must be some warning signs indicating the problems that it faces. Action must be taken immediately to prevent project failure.
These are the top ten reasons why projects fail. Now that you have the information, you should start considering what you

can do to avoid this failure. This can consist of proper training for team members, use of project management software, or simply being more transparent. There are a lot of tools that can help prevent project failure. Find what works for you and your team, and give your project a higher chance of success.

Chapter 13: Ten Tips for Successful Project Management

Managing a project to its successful completion requires a project manager who is able to see the bigger picture and stay proactive. A good project manager will always be quick to encourage his team and treat every member with the respect they deserve. Effective communication is very important as well as acknowledging the accomplishments of the people you work with.

The bottom line is that become a better project manager isn't just about what you do, but also how you go about doing it. If you can create the right synergy and atmosphere within your team, they will respond positively to your leadership. Here are ten tips that can help you do this:

1. See the bigger picture

A project manager must always be able to fix their eyes on the big picture. It is critical for project success that you keep every outcome in perspective, knowing fully where you are headed and how you intend to arrive at your destination. Understand how every decision you make right now will affect the current and future situation of your project. Another thing to remember is that sharing your vision with your team will make your work a lot easier.

2. Avoid making unnecessary assumptions

Always investigate to determine what the real facts are before you make a decision. Making assumptions shouldn't be the normal procedure when handling project issues. Resort to using assumptions only as the last option so as to avoid taking unwarranted risks that might jeopardize the project. The more you get used to dealing with facts rather than assumptions, the more confident you become in your abilities.

3. Develop a "Can Do" attitude

A project manager will always run into problems once in a while. No project is perfect and challenges crop up from time to time. It is important that you see every problem as a challenge that needs to be overcome. Moaning and complaining will not help you one bit. The challenges aren't meant to break you but to build you up. Developing a "can do" attitude will help you stay flexible, creative, and resolute so that every challenge is accepted as an opportunity to make you a better project manager.

4. Always communicate clearly

Are you the kind of person who says what they mean and means what they say? As a project manager, clear communication is important because people need to know exactly what you are saying. Effective communication means giving your team the right information at the right time.

You have to give them information that will enable them to perform their assignments to the best of their abilities. Let them know what is required of them rather than assuming that they already know. Effective and clear communication will ensure support from stakeholders and team members. It will also help people identify problems early and make better decisions. The working relationships within the project will also be strengthened.

Some project managers think that the less clear they are, the more room they have to maneuver. The problem with this kind of thinking is that being vague opens the door for confusion, misunderstanding, and errors.

5. Always ask "Why" questions

When someone makes a request or acts in a particular manner, always investigate the reasons why. If you can understand why people do what they do, you will be better able to respond to your project team and stakeholders, thus motivating them more. Once you determine the reasons why a particular action was taken, share the information with others.

6. Be as detailed as possible

It is your responsibility as project manager to thoroughly examine any project issues that arise. You know what the project plan contains, and you have to be able to describe this plan in details to those concerned with implementing it. If people can understand the intended results of the project, they will find it easier to visualize the benefits of the project. For example, people may complete the assignments given simply because you have told them to do so. However, if you take the time to explain the project benefits, then you are likely to get a much more serious commitment from them.

Clarity makes a huge difference in the way people handle

their tasks within a project environment. The clearer you are with what is required, the more insightful your team will be when dealing with project issues. This ultimately motivates people to perform better and minimizes the likelihood of errors being made.

7. Get people on your side

It is extremely counterproductive to treat people like enemies rather than allies. You should always strive to focus on the things you have in common instead of looking at individual agendas. When you view people as allies, you will act positively toward them. The result is that people will be encouraged to open up and be more creative in developing and implementing new ideas. Brainstorming is a crucial tool in a project, and people need to feel comfortable around and appreciated by their project manager. On the other hand, if you see and treat people as adversaries, you will alienate them and make them more defensive.

8. Recognize good performance

If a team member does good work, acknowledge their performance by letting them know how much you appreciate it. Let their colleagues and superiors know about it as well. By doing so, you will let the person know that their value within the team is recognized and appreciated. This conscious effort to acknowledge good performance will motivate people such that they will even want to work with you on other projects in the future.

In the initial stages of a project, the team members will be highly motivated. However, as weeks go by, their motivation will start to wane if you do not offer regular encouragement. People generally want to be informed of their performance for three reasons:

- It gives them personal satisfaction knowing that they have achieved milestones.

- Acknowledging their good performance lets them know that they are on track.

- It will strengthen their belief in their ability to attain the project's final goals.

Recognizing good performance must involve mentioning the specific actions they took that deserve praise. The feedback should also be given as quickly as possible rather than weeks later. Establish intermediate milestones that will make it easier to track and assess the performance of your team members.

9. Be respectful
A project manager should always try to appreciate people's efforts. The truth is that not all your team members will perform at a high level, and some will have more weaknesses than others. However, nobody is born without strengths. It is, therefore, important that you focus on the strengths of your people instead of highlighting their weaknesses all the time. Everyone has a quality that you can respect and people will actually be extra motivated when they know that they are respected by their colleagues.

10. Exercise management as well as leadership
Management and leadership may be related but they are also two very distinct approaches when it comes to guiding and supporting people. A good project manager must learn how to act as a manager and a leader.

A manager focuses on systems, processes, and information. They create a plan and evaluate performance. They expect a semblance of order and efficiency from their team and ensure that the necessary support structures are in place to achieve excellent results. Management is oriented towards the what, when, and how of achieving project objectives. It also involves informing people about project progress and handling whatever challenges that may arise.

On the other hand, a leader focuses more on the people they work with. They try to share their vision for the project and inject some excitement into the team. A leader also goes out of their way to encourage the team to achieve excellent results. Leadership tends to orient towards the why of a project. People are more likely to buy into and commit to the project if they understand the significance of the project. A leader also takes the time to acknowledge the contributions individuals make towards the success of the project.

Conclusion

Most people you talk to will tell you that getting a project to succeed is not an easy prospect. It requires a high level of expertise, experience, knowledge, skill and effort. A project needs adequate resources to ensure that all the project activities flow as smoothly as possible. There are also many risks and uncertainties to deal with.

This book has shown you that the basic principles that guide project management are quite simple. Not easy, but simple. The information you have obtained from this book will help you effectively and efficiently plan and manage your project, regardless of size, type, scope, or geographical location. The guidelines specified in this book will enable you to deal with the myriad of challenges that project managers face on the job every day.

However, having the knowledge in your head is one thing – applying it is a totally different matter. You need to take this knowledge and practice it. If need be, read the book again to remind yourself of the techniques to use to succeed in project management.

It is our hope that you have gained enough information here to successfully manage any kind of project. From now on, you should be able to face any challenge in life by thinking and behaving like a project manager!

Made in the USA
San Bernardino, CA
16 March 2017